Understanding 10–11-Year-Olds

Understanding Your Child Series

The Tavistock Clinic has an international reputation as a centre of excellence for training, clinical mental health work, research and scholarship. Written by professionals working in the Child and Family and the Adolescent Departments, the guides in this series present balanced and sensitive advice that will help adults to become, or to feel that they are, "good enough" parents. Each book concentrates on a key transition in a child's life from birth to adolescence, looking especially at how parents' emotions and experiences interact with those of their children. The titles in the Understanding Your Child series are essential reading for new and experienced parents, relatives, friends and carers, as well as for the multi-agency professionals who are working to support children and their families.

also in the series

Understanding Your Baby
Sophie Boswell
ISBN 978 1 84310 242 7

Understanding Your One-Year-Old
Sarah Gustavus Jones
ISBN 978 1 84310 241 0

Understanding Your Two-Year-Old
Lisa Miller
ISBN 978 1 84310 288 5

Understanding Your Three-Year-Old
Louise Emanuel
ISBN 978 1 84310 243 4

Understanding 4–5-Year-Olds
Lesley Maroni
ISBN 978 1 84310 534 3

Understanding 6–7-Year-Olds
Corinne Aves
ISBN 978 1 84310 467 4

Understanding 8–9-Year-Olds
Biddy Youell
ISBN 978 1 84310 673 9

Understanding 12–14-Year-Olds
Margot Waddell
ISBN 978 1 84310 367 7

Understanding Your Young Child with Special Needs
Pamela Bartram
ISBN 978 1 84310 533 6

Understanding
10–11-Year-Olds

Rebecca Bergese

Jessica Kingsley Publishers
London and Philadelphia

First published in 2008
by Jessica Kingsley Publishers
116 Pentonville Road
London N1 9JB, UK
and
400 Market Street, Suite 400
Philadelphia, PA 19106, USA

www.jkp.com

Library of Congress Cataloging in Publication Data
Bergese, Rebecca.
  Understanding 10-11-year-olds / Rebecca Bergese.
    p. cm.
  ISBN 978-1-84310-674-6 (pb : alk. paper) 1. Child psychology. 2. Child development. I.
Title. II. Title: Understanding ten-eleven year olds.
  BF721.B3667 2008
  155.42'4--dc22
                              2008001895

British Library Cataloguing in Publication Data
A CIP catalogue record for this book is available from the British Library

ISBN 978 1 84310 674 6

Printed and bound in the United States by
Thomson-Shore, 7300 Joy Road, Dexter, MI 48130

Contents

Acknowledgements

I am indebted to all the parents and children who through personal or professional contact have contributed so much to the content of this book. Thank you particularly to my daughters, who may find some of these ideas familiar.

Foreword

The Tavistock Clinic has an international reputation as a centre of excellence for training, clinical mental health work, research and scholarship. Established in 1920, its history is one of groundbreaking work. The original aim of the Clinic was to offer treatment which could be used as the basis of research into the social prevention and treatment of mental health problems, and to teach these emerging skills to other professionals. Later work turned towards the treatment of trauma, the understanding of conscious and unconscious processes in groups, as well as important and influential work in developmental psychology. Work in perinatal bereavement led to a new understanding within the medical profession of the experience of stillbirth, and of the development of new forms of support for mourning parents and families. The development in the 1950s and 1960s of a systemic model of psychotherapy, focusing on the interaction between children and parents and within families, has grown into the substantial body of theoretical knowledge and therapeutic techniques used in the Tavistock's training and research in family therapy.

The Understanding Your Child series has an important place in the history of the Tavistock Clinic. It has been issued in a completely new form three times: in the 1960s, the 1990s, and in 2004. Each time the authors, drawing on their clinical background and specialist training, have set out to reflect on the extraordinary story of "ordinary development" as it was observed and experienced at the time. Society changes, of course, and so has this series, as it attempts to make sense of everyday accounts of the ways in which a developing child interacts with his or her parents, carers and the wider world. But within this changing scene there has been something constant, and it is best described as a continuing enthusiasm for a view of development which recognizes the importance of the strong feelings and emotions experienced at each stage of development.

This book focuses on 10–11-year-olds, the age when children are no longer little and "finally" reach the coveted double figures. Children at this age start to become more aware of the adult world and often want to start to take part in it. They experience growing independence, yet at the same time are very committed to belonging to one kind of group or another. Rebecca Bergese covers issues pertinent to parents and professionals such as how to support children at this age while giving them more freedom, children's feelings about changes happening to their body, and school life and bullying behaviour. She offers sound advice on how to support children in moving on from this crossroads into adolescence.

Jonathan Bradley
Child Psychotherapist
General Editor of the Understanding Your Child Series

Introduction

Sitting with her back to me, I can see a tall girl with long well-brushed blonde hair. Sitting comfortably on the edge of her front garden wall, she is waiting for her mother to arrive home. She wears fashionably frayed and worn jeans with a pink T-shirt. The outfit is finished off with a striped short skirt clinging to her jeans and a number of silver necklaces and long swinging earrings. Erin is fiddling with a collection of small items in her lap. Stepping closer I see that she is trying to untangle several metal objects – a comb, a kitten, a diamante heart, a dolphin, a furry squirrel and a wooden map of Africa, all key rings attached to her school bag. Turning to me she explains that she wants to sort them out as she has so many now that her school bag is getting heavy. The key ring collection hangs like a bunch of medals from a chain, trophies of her summer holiday trips to amusement parks, a friend's birthday party or a family seaside holiday. Erin gives me a dazzling smile and as if taking me into her confidence, she goes on to tell me that she will need a new bag for the coming year as this one is no longer big enough. "Will we have lockers do you think?" she asks me, as if searching knowledge acquired from extensive research watching television programmes about "High School". I tell her that I think she will have a locker at her new school but I don't know if she will find time to use it as she goes from one lesson to another. Erin notices my bag and asks about my family. She is curious, wondering what 16-year-olds like to do with their free time. As I continue on my way home, her mother arrives to open the front door.

A group of boys proceed along the pavement nearby, an untidy impression of many large feet and long legs turning four boys into ten. Their bodies lean forward with eager physicality, almost tense with expectation as they half

11

push, half kick a squashed ball along the street. Without being noisy their voices, like their feet, expand in the space, creating the illusion of a crowd as they call out encouragement to each other. As they pass me, however, their voices drop in volume and their bodies slow in a gesture of caution. Among them is a smaller dark-haired boy with pale skin, intent on his account of his afternoon's football at his friend's birthday party. He instinctively joins with his friends in checking his enthusiasm and the volume of his tone as they approach me on the street. I turn towards them with a smile, only to meet four averted heads and an impression of velvety hilltops, as they all sport cropped haircuts. One boy and his friend plan to meet later at the end of the street to carry on their tournament of penalty shots in the park, as long as they can gather enough cash to buy a new football. Another boy is confident and assured in his announcement that they need not worry, his dad has a jar full of small change at home and he can borrow enough for them to get a new ball at the corner shop. Their afternoon looks set to be a good one.

Erin glances momentarily at them before shaking her hair out of her eyes and following her mother into the house at a discreet distance.

Becoming "two figures"

Once children go to school and begin to count and to grasp the names and meanings of numbers, they often look forward eagerly to the time when they will be 10 years old – double figures! To a seven- or eight-year-old the 10- and 11-year-old represents maturity, knowledge and self-possession. The 11-year-old is awarded a degree of independence that superficially lends high status. Our adult perspective may be utterly different, but for the 11-year-olds themselves, it is an era that can be either happily straightforward or the dawn of more complicated feelings, as we will explore in this book.

The following chapters are intended to focus on the outlook of children who are no longer little, having instead to acquire skills and a perspective that are not so distant from the views they will hold as an adult later. This view of 10- and 11-year-olds is based on the understanding and theoretical thinking of psychoanalysts such as Sigmund Freud, Melanie Klein, Wilfred Bion and Donald Winnicott, all of whom developed their ideas from extensive professional experience of adults and children. It is not a guide or a handbook as such, but rather an account of a 10- or 11-year-old's world, and connecting it to a developing emotional life. Drawing on the ideas of psychoanalytic writers, this book begins from the premise that our emotions are an intrinsic part of our lives, and that our feelings often powerfully influence other elements of our being such as our physical health and our ability to think and understand the world around us.

The children in the opening paragraphs are all turning 11, coming to the end of their time in primary school and looking forward to the celebrations before the long summer holiday. The imminent change to the bigger second-ary school, in which they will have to start as the "little" ones at the bottom all over again, stirs up mixed responses in both. Some of their friends have older brothers and sisters, and so any transitions are experiences they have been able to witness second hand throughout their growing years. Perhaps there is a relief and pleasure in slowly being able to join the club of older children. Some, like Erin, are the oldest child in their family. With two younger sisters, Erin feels that she is lucky to be growing up and looks forward eagerly to being a teenager and being able to choose her own clothes and listen to music on a portable media player, or have her own mobile phone. For other girls of 10, the days are easy and fun, meeting with other girls to go swimming or sharing pictures they have collected from girls' magazines of their favourite boy band or celebrity models, or unself-consciously enjoying membership of a specialist skills group such as riding or playing in a local orchestra. The idea of growing and one day taking on the interests and activities of the older girls they meet is far away from their minds. More fun to join in with a local fund-raising walk to raise awareness of the hole in the ozone layer, and let adults carry on with the day-to-day worry of how to earn enough money or manage Granddad's forgetfulness.

These snapshot portraits give a flavour of the 10- and 11-year-old. The following pages explore the world of the child who is leaving behind the early years' experience, greatly coloured by home and family, and beginning to move out into a more independent self-aware perspective and to tackle a wider, deeper challenge than before. In trying to grasp the outlook of a child in this age group, we can imagine the worries and concerns as well as the delights and pleasures of children at this point in their lives; in so doing, we have a resource to call on should difficulties arise.

As with every age group there are endless individual developments and each child will be at their own developmental stage whatever their chronolog-ical age, but the likelihood of a changeable outlook and a huge variation in emotional, physical and mental maturity is characteristic of this group of youngsters. This is most evident when visiting a school class of 10-year-olds. You will see a room of young people, some small and slender, quite like children of seven or eight, but you will also encounter tall, almost adolescent girls and boys, some physically pubertal with signs of their bodies changing, others tall and gangling, laughing and clowning around in the class. It is sometimes hard to imagine that they can all be the same age.

Although this is not the era of the adolescent, perhaps the most noticeable characteristic of children in this group is their commitment to a bigger group in that they will most likely enjoy being an established member of one kind of group or another, but simultaneously they are striving to make sense of their growing awareness of an identity and ultimately an independent life.

1

Family Life

Nowadays, children are likely to be familiar with a whole variety of family compositions. At school they will meet children who may have one parent, or both, or a combination of carers, same sex or otherwise. It is no longer inevitable that children will feel different if their family does not consist of mother and father and a sibling or two. Rather, they might feel a kind of solidarity and normality in having a family that is a mixture of all age groups. Children of 10 and 11 will have had contact with others from many family compositions both in school and socially. Some will be living with parents and have done so all their lives, while others will have memories of a time with two birth parents but now live in another situation. The influence of family and family life on children is enormous and no less so for this age group. How it influences them, and the extent to which family are a resource for children, will depend a great deal on the combination of previous experiences and their own innate outlook on the world.

Because any number of family constellations will be familiar to many children, we must be cautious in making assumptions about a child's view of their own family's security and resilience. Some children have an innate sense of themselves and their space in the world, which will assist them in coping with all manner of family or life changes, while others will feel unsure and doubtful about how to weather even quite ordinary shifts and events in the family's life. More confusingly, 10- and 11-year-olds may not display signs of vulnerability or anxiety as a younger child might do, because they have already had to construct ways of managing a whole range of feelings in order to flourish in groups away from their families. It would be relatively unusual for a 10-year-old to show concern about a parent's absence through direct bodily clinging, or for feelings of insecurity to be expressed verbally or through passionate confrontation.

Mother and father

Without doubt the most significant relationships in the young child's life will be with his or her mother and father even if the child is not cared for by them. In the early weeks and months of life, infants are entirely dependent on their mother to keep them alive and as we know from observation, the bond between mother and baby is potentially very strong, whether or not they would later feel themselves to be close. Throughout the developing years mother and child are engaged in a separating process in preparation for eventual physical independence. This occurs most evidently in our conscious efforts to assist our children in managing the world through skilled behaviours and social communication. It takes place less obviously in terms of our attitudes, our expectations and our enjoyment of the world, which will also influence their development physically, intellectually and psychologically.

A fine balance has to be achieved between encouraging a sense of resourcefulness and strength and yet continuing to offer children safety and emotional support until they are truly ready to manage alone. The progress of this development will be influenced to an extent by the mother's and father's own early experience as well as their personality, and their relationship as a couple. In fact, the emotional task this requires is quite a challenge, often stirring up troubling feelings of anger or loss when we least expect them.

When a child first attends playgroup, nursery or school, the parents can find themselves quite thrown by the distracting feelings that are swimming around. Many mothers report waiting eagerly to return to work after maternity leave, or when their child is starting school, only to spend the first days feeling utterly lost and completely unable to think about their work. To a lesser extent the same dilemmas and conflicts of feeling will still be around with 10- and 11-year-olds, as older children begin to identify more with their friends or other youngsters of their age group. Their relationship with their parent or carer is subtly changing. This is often complicated by the huge variation in physical development of children at this time. A 10-year-old girl may be on the cusp of puberty and appear quite grown-up for her age, but emotionally she continues to want the closeness and reassurance of playing at home, taking part in games that she has enjoyed in recent years. It might be easy to think that this 10-year-old is ready to go out with her friends alone, or to take responsibility for herself, joining in with family concerns, but she is not yet able to deal with the complex feelings that accompany this more adult lifestyle.

Miranda, aged 10, was in the last year of her primary school, when she started to feel uncomfortable about the increasing interest of the other girls in her class in cosmetics and fashionable clothes. Some of them talked in an excited giggly way about the boys in class, and about their interest in the older boys at the nearby secondary school. They mildly teased Miranda because she did not want to join in with these speculative conversations and preferred reading books or going to the local nature-watching club. Naturally tall, with long legs and beautiful olive skin, Miranda had all the appearance of a young teenager. Her large brown eyes and slender frame made her the envy of some of her classmates, who could not resist teasing her about her attractiveness. Miranda felt confused and overwhelmed by these suggestions and at home she became increasingly determined to engage her parents' attention, insisting that they join her in board games or watch Disney films with her in the evenings.

At first her mother was pleased by the closeness between Miranda and herself, but as the days passed, her mother noticed a kind of inflexibility in Miranda, and the playing became rather a chore on a busy weekday evening, with household work to be done. It was a puzzling development as Miranda seemed so mature and responsible, often helping her mother with household activities and seeming such a mild, easy-going young girl. Her mother remembered her own transition to secondary school then, and how she had felt very worried about the pressure of adolescence and scared by the changes taking place in her body. She understood then that Miranda's sudden interest in home life and playing with toys was probably also connected to worries about the future. Miranda was hoping to stave off the challenging developments of mind and body that inevitably lay ahead.

As they had always been able to chat together, Miranda's mother was able to talk to her and offer her some time to revisit the games of her earlier years, while also spending time with Miranda and taking an interest in the clothes and activities of older girls they both knew. Although it was difficult to be patient, Miranda's mother could see that only patience would offer Miranda reassurance and a sense that there was no need to hurry towards adolescence, nor yet to retreat to the outlook of a much younger child. At the same time, Miranda's mother could offer her a safe space to explore in the form of watching films together or talking about mother's own secondary school experience so that Miranda could gain confidence away from the comments of peers.

This example shows how very important the relationship with the mother or a close carer can be, but unlike earlier times, one's importance is not so evident and immediate. Many 10- and 11-year-olds will feel quite able and keen to spend a bit of time away from the family with friends, or joining in activities that offer them a degree of separateness and privacy from the gaze of their mother and father. Parents can feel grateful, as it allows a little space for their own interests and friends. Sometimes they can feel surprised and hurt by a 10-year-old's growing independence and as at all stages of childhood, can be caught out by the sudden spurt of growth and change.

Parents may have been accustomed to spending weekends with their children, keeping them company at a distance while they play with computer games, or dress up dolls, or sort through their trading card collections, or build intricate models of space ships. For many families these are the golden days enjoyed by everyone in the group. Then, we find that they no longer want us to go with them to play in the park. Suddenly it is not Mum or Dad who are the most desirable companions with whom all pleasures and pains are shared. This will take some adjustment when one has enjoyed the companionable years of young childhood. If parents or carers are surprised by this development, it is then quite easy to miss the more subtle requests for love and support. Naturally the support and companionship offered will need a careful assessment of the real circumstances, the child's personality, and our own resources. As previously mentioned, a carer's response will be partly influenced by his or her own family life as a child.

It is important to mention cultural differences too. Most children in this age group will have strikingly different experiences of growing up from their parents. Sometimes this is obvious when families emigrate, leaving their indigenous culture to settle in a new, often economically more secure environment. Parents may have endured hardship and grown up in a very different culture psychologically. In western culture there is a prevailing attitude that childhood is a time of innocence and a time in which the growing person will be protected from specific injustices and pressures.

The view of children may take a different shape in other cultures. Families often feel a conflict, wanting their children to benefit from the security of the new culture, but feeling doubtful about the moral impact of this on their developing youngsters. This is a complex matter and not one to expand on here, except to say that naturally, parents may have mixed feelings when confronted by their 10- or 11-year-olds' insistence on a degree of independence. Our capacity to help our children with this development will rely on our own sense of comfort and ease in our environment. If we are living far from our families and feel that we do not have friends and relatives to contact, then it can be hard to feel confident that our children will benefit from contact with a larger world. But there is no doubt that helping our children to make tentative steps towards relationships with other adults, as well as children at school and in their family, will help them to develop confidence and a sense of belonging in the wider world not only at school but also later in work and more intimate relationships.

Mothers

Where does the mother fit into the imagination of children in this group? By implication, the mother is viewed with a more complicated set of thoughts and emotions than previously, and the home circumstances will contribute to the sense of a mother's identity in a child's mind. Even in the most adverse circumstances, and on occasions when a mother, for reasons of health or misfortune, is unable to be with her child, there is plenty of evidence to show us that children not only have a strong sense of their mother's identity but also have a strong attachment to her. By attachment, I am referring to a bond or a link, though not inevitably a loving one. The bond may be formed of complicated mixtures of affectionate or quite angry bitter feelings sometimes.

The significant point is that there is a deep connection between a pre-pubertal child and his or her mother. By this age, children will have started to make comparisons between the relative assets and qualities of one mother and another, but also less consciously perhaps, children will be forming a view of their own identity in relation to the picture they have of their mother. If a boy finds his mother to be kind, indulgent, easy-going, this will begin to contribute to his sense of himself in the present, but it will shape a sense of the identity he may have as a man. This experience may lend itself to the forging of a sense of himself as a likeable, effective, influential person, or alternatively one whom it is difficult to resist and limit.

Either way, a child of this age will have a mother in mind who cannot be substituted by another mother or family member. She may or may not be the subject of quite strong feelings of attachment, perhaps mixed with confusing dreams of staying with her and being her chosen companion, despite the real presence of an adult father or other partner. This can apply to girls as much as to boys. At times it may be connected to worries or pressure that is present in the child's life. At other times, by contrast, the mother exists as a strange hybrid creature who is needed and loved, but not viewed as a fully rounded person with a life of her own, or views of her own. Real-life events that seem to contradict this fact can be met with a sulky and irritable response. Perhaps the most likely shape for a mother as seen by a 10-year-old is one of an enduring reliable figure who nevertheless seems overly concerned with order and hygiene!

On the whole, however, children at this time will be more conscious of the reality of the world and will benefit from the knowledge of their mother's presence somewhere not too distant, although they will be largely unaware of this need themselves. This perspective is captured by Enid Blyton in her books for children. The heroes and heroines of the Famous Five series, for instance, are engaged in daring adventures, using their knowledge and wit to pursue bad characters of many kinds. In each tale, however, their days are punctuated by the presence of mother, who is busy with household activities somewhere in the background, but who provides the essential resources, in the form of sandwiches or the camping equipment they will need if they are to set forth on their latest mission. Nowadays, mothers are likely to have rather busier and more colourful lives than Enid Blyton's fictional mother, but for most 10- and 11-year-olds, the picture will endure: mothers are engaged in some uninteresting adult activity which keeps them out of trouble while their children are occupied with exciting imaginary feats.

Fathers

Fathers are very important in the lives of 10- and 11-year-olds. This fact may be greeted with mixed feelings by parents and carers, not least fathers themselves. Whereas mothers are so crucial from the early weeks and months of life, fathers too will have a vital part in their child's emotional development from the earliest days, whether or not they are present in the lives of their offspring. Quite often in a world which sees women taking on more and more of the responsibilities and working roles that were once male preserves, there can be an associated feeling that mothers and fathers are largely interchangeable. In some respects this is true enough, and we can see a huge variation in the way parents share out their care of their children. Parents who can enjoy the benefit of sharing the upbringing of the children will be able to model a cooperative and adaptable relationship between the sexes from which children can draw in their own relationships later.

Same-sex couples are equally able to provide this opportunity for their children, as it is not so much a matter of gender as the modelling of collaborative functioning. Sharing may be interpreted in numerous ways by parents, sometimes leading parents to question whether any aspect of parenting can or should be allotted to one sex or the other. As a consequence, there is growing concern about how fathers can establish a positive and significant contribution in the lives of their children. This doubt seems an unfortunate extension of a general tendency in recent times to overlook positive masculine qualities.

Both boys and girls in this age group will already have formed a clear idea of themselves in relation to their families. Whether children have ever had contact with their father or not, notions of their origins and what kind of family they belong to will have been clearly formed.

This is evident even in the lives of children who have never known their birth parents, or who have no knowledge of their origins. Sometimes this allows the child to build helpful ideas about qualities or strengths they would like to have: being good at sport, being brave, growing very tall and strong, like the imagined parent. Sometimes the absence of a man who can be identified as father leads to feelings of doubt and worry. Usually this can be dispelled if children feel free to ask or to talk about the absent individual. Sometimes, the absence of the actual father is not important because the child finds other male figures to look to and to help him or her form ideas about what a father might be.

> This was Etem's experience. He was the only son of his mother, who had become pregnant when she was 17. The relationship with Etem's father did not withstand the pressure of the pregnancy on their young lives, and the couple soon drifted apart. Luckily his mother was well supported by her own parents, who were determined to help their daughter to give her baby the best chance in life. Etem grew up with his mother, but was cared for much of the week by his grandparents. Etem also spent time with his aunts and uncles, who were his mother's younger siblings, still living at home. Although Etem's father was never mentioned and he had little contact with the family, Etem grew up in a happy secure family, enjoying his place as the "baby" even when he was quite a big boy. He had the thoughtful attention of his grandfather, who encouraged Etem to build both

physical and social confidence by taking him on regular delivery runs in his van, taking customers their deliveries of fruit and vegetables. Etem enjoyed this relationship with his grandfather, feeling that he had a friendly and reliable grown-up who demonstrated that he could get on in life and find encouragement and gratitude for his masculine qualities.

Later when Etem started to want to be with his friends and felt torn between Granddad and a trip to football, his grandfather was able to encourage Etem in his new sport and took an interest in his weekly practice. One can see that Granddad provided Etem with a very satisfactory substitute, especially as he was young enough and fit enough to be a strong physical presence, joining in with football and cricket. Only much later, when Etem was almost adult himself, did he begin to wonder about his real father. Because Etem and Granddad had a long-standing and affectionate relationship, Granddad and his mother were able to talk to him about whether he wanted to make contact with his father, without feeling surprised or resentful that Etem needed to put aside Granddad in his curiosity about his origins.

Boys of 10 and 11 vary hugely in their size and development. At around this age, they are more conscious of their masculinity in a more realistic sense. As younger boys they identify with stereotypical ideas of masculinity: exceptional physical strength, courage, heroic endurance, fearlessness in the face of adversity. In the past they would have been enthralled by comic book heroes and tales of explorers. Nowadays boys find similar heroes in the characters in video games or television programmes and sporting celebrities. In their younger years their admiration is based on a need to have a very clearly defined sense of a champion or hero with which to identify, but by 10, children are more aware of the real world and more conscious of the complexity and uncertainty that might face men in day-to-day life. For the first time perhaps they are conscious of the challenge that might face their fathers or other male figures in the real life of their family. This discovery can lead to complicated feelings. Children look to their father as a version of a hero, whether or not this view has any correspondence with the parents' personalities or culture. A boy or girl of 10 may feel they need to hold on to the imaginary picture of a superhero Dad, who will ensure that good prevails and can be relied on to keep them safe. Simultaneously, they are increasingly conscious of the reality of the adult world through personal experience, through television and films, and from a developing consciousness of reality.

They may struggle with the realization of their father being fallible and try to keep this consciousness at bay.

Other children will feel concern about the discovery of their own critical awareness of a parent. Most children will find support and gain confidence from being able to watch and learn how their fathers deal with problems of the real world.

Some boys will wish to be a helpful associate to the adult man in the family and become involved in quasi-adult activities. This can be the case when one hears of younger boys starting on a chapter of mildly delinquent behaviour. At first they are motivated by the worrying sense of helplessness that comes from a better understanding of the difficulties a family may have to deal with, for example loss of income with unemployment. It may be quite upsetting to a boy of this age that he is not yet physically or emotionally mature enough to be able to make a significant contribution.

> Reece was determined to try to find a way to help his mother and stepfather when his mother lost her job. He knew that without her income, the family would have few resources to survive on. He felt resentful and angry with his stepfather for not rescuing the family from worry. Then he began to feel angry and resentful about everyone who wasn't suffering as he and his family were. This in turn prevented him from talking to anyone, and so his angry feelings mounted inside him. By chance, he discovered that a foreign coin he had found in the street fitted exactly into the slot in the parking meters outside his school. Out of curiosity he put the coin into the meter, thinking that perhaps he could find a way to cheat the meters and save his mother some money. Unfortunately, the foreign coin fell down into the slot but immediately jammed the mechanism, causing the meter to break. Reece was disappointed but then felt rather pleased with himself. The jammed machine would cause annoyance and inconvenience to all the parents arriving at school the next day.
>
> For a few moments Reece enjoyed the thrill and sense of power this gave him, contrasting sharply with the combined sense of being small and futile that he experienced at home each day. Without the understanding and help of his stepfather, Reece could feel indignant and justified in his mildly destructive behaviour. It was a lucky coincidence that Reece's stepfather had a younger cousin who like Reece had been mischievous and destructive in his young teenage years. Reece's stepfather had collected his cousin from the police station on a number

of occasions and knew about this kind of naughtiness. When Reece was caught by one of his teachers, who phoned home, Reece's mother and stepfather were able to talk to him and wanted to find out what was worrying him. The shared discussion which followed helped Reece to see that he was loved by his family and that they valued him despite his age and lack of earnings. To his surprise he started to feel calmer and hopeful about the future at home.

Grandparents and the wider family

By the time a child is 10 or 11, connections will probably have been long established with other relatives. This may provide a net of adults to whom parents and children can relate. Grandparents can be very influential in the lives of their 10- and 11-year-old grandchildren, and this can be advantageous or otherwise for the children and their carers.

Nowadays, families are less likely to live close to relatives and often grandparents or other extended family members are not close enough for regular contact with children. Nevertheless, a relationship of whatever kind will have evolved and usually contributes to a child's outlook and expectations to some extent.

Hasan lived in a large city with his mother Laura in a small one bedroom flat. His mum had to work long hours to be able to support them both, having moved away from her partner when Hasan was three years old. Her family and Hasan's father remained in the provincial town where Laura had been born, and felt rather injured and surprised by her decision to start a new life two hours' train journey away from them. For Laura, the move was an essential kick-start to a new life and for her to leave the past behind, but in doing so she left behind the immediate contact with her own mother and father.

Laura soon found herself a steady job in a city business and enjoyed the sense of independence it offered. Luckily she was able to find good childcare for Hasan and when he was older he attended an inner city school with good childcare support for working families. Hasan thrived in the busy, lively environment and enjoyed the company of other children, responding to the warm easy-going care of teachers and adults in the after-school club he attended. He liked talking to his grandmother and grandfather on the phone and later, when they bought a computer, he could send them emails. On the surface things were comfortable and Laura's parents adjusted to their daughter's way of life, even though it caused them some sadness and worry about the safety of life in the city. Laura and her parents did not always share the same values for Hasan, and she felt that they were quite critical of her parenting. In fact they were feeling all the concern that would be natural for parents, and also for grandparents. They so wanted to give Hasan a bit of the life they had been able to provide for his mother. So they invited Hasan to come and stay in the school holidays, hoping to redress the balance.

When Hasan did stay with his grandparents as a little boy, he enjoyed the walks through the wood looking for conkers, or wading in the streams trying to build dams, or climbing up the trees near his grandparents' home. They were able to indulge him in a way that his mum could not, taking him on trips to the nearby zoo, or letting him stay up in the evenings to play computer games with his grandpa. But as he grew older, Hasan began to have more activities that kept him at home in the holiday and though not yet adolescent, his interests were moving on. When his grandma phoned, he was not always at home, and her cheerful enquiries about football teams or school trips became annoying. Typically Hasan found himself in a halfway place. He was very attached to his grandparents and fondly remembered some of the rituals of staying with them, and he did enjoy the trees and space of their rural home. At the age of 10 he was now thinking about the challenges of growing up and wanting adventures, whether real or imaginary, that would help him to test out his abilities to cope alone. He and his friends talked about taking trips together, and although he knew that this would not be permitted by their families, he felt uncomfortable to be reminded of his attachment and dependence on his warm-hearted relatives.

This kind of dilemma takes place within children without them really being aware of it. Instead it can show itself in a tendency to become more reticent and reserved with aunts and grandmothers while becoming more actively engaged in hobbies and social exchanges with the peer group. With help from friends, Hasan's grandparents recognized this change in Hasan and so did not continue to feel puzzled or rejected by his less enthusiastic telephone conversations, and fewer visits than before. But when the summer holiday arrived, they invited Hasan to come with a friend and arranged a camping trip for the boys, joining a local club supervised by a professional worker. This allowed Hasan to keep hold of some of the old pleasures of having his grandparents' attention, while not having to cut them off in the effort to build a new alterna-tive life with his friends. Without this kind of understanding from grandpar-ents and other older relatives, children of this age can feel torn, not wanting to hurt the feelings of loved relatives, but wanting to strengthen their sense of independence. It is hard too for an 11-year-old to imagine that grandparents were once children too. As younger children they can achieve this more easily, imagining that people are essentially preoccupied by the same interests and concerns, but by 10 they feel a sense of history. They can now recall the past, the time of their infancy, and feel that they have progressed so far, doubtful perhaps that adults can appreciate or observe just what an enormous journey has already been undertaken.

Sometimes life at home can be stressful for both adults and children, par-ticularly at times of change such as illness or unemployment. Lesser, more subtle change is also taking place as 10-year-old children develop a height-ened awareness of the complexity of real life. Unlike the child of two years earlier, they can begin to face the ordinary difficulties of life with a greater understanding of the intricacies. Instead of trying to create a secure manage-able world in their imagination, an alternative empire perhaps, governed by strict rules imposed by themselves or their group of friends, the 10- or 11-year-old will start to apply a more experienced reasoning. If things have gone well, they will now be able to read more complicated books and to follow arguments put forward by adults, teachers, television presenters and so on and gather some of this experience to bring to their own thinking. While favourite books, television programmes and DVDs will probably still draw on the action adventures and heroes and demons of both classic and contempo-rary culture, the appeal of *Star Wars* or *Buffy the Vampire Slayer* or *Lord of the Rings* will be slightly different. For someone of 11, the emotional dilemmas and complexities in real life can be contemplated. At the same time this can take place only within the secure knowledge that these explorations are hypo-thetical and parents or carers are still available to deal with the management of everyday life.

A generation gap

Not yet adolescent, the 11-year-old is interested in a separate life, though, and this can be both exciting or worrying depending on the home circumstances. When families are under a lot of pressure, from marital tension or serious illness for example, it is hard to find time for children's worries that may seem slight by comparison. This was what happened to Ioan.

Ioan was the middle child of busy, hard-working parents who lived in a small town. Life was not easy, but steady for the family, with both parents working hard, though his mum was always home to look after him and his brother and baby sister after school. Ioan had grown up with friends who lived in the same street and his family counted themselves lucky that they had a good network of friends and neighbours. He and his friend Gary joined the Cub Scouts together when they were seven and he often spent time in Gary's house or with his grandmother, who lived close by.

Unfortunately, Ioan's mother became seriously ill with a chronic disease and had to take prolonged sick leave. This put an unexpected strain on the family, as everyone was worried about Mum, and because she could not work, her income was reduced as the weeks of her illness accumulated. At last, the doctors announced that the disease was under control and she would make good progress and soon be able to return to work. During her illness everyone had been very supportive and offered to help her husband with household work and looking after the three children. Grandmother had also been a huge help as she could look after the children for a while when Dad was still at work. During this time, Ioan was relieved to have his friendship with Gary and the chance to go to the park or ride his bike. He and Gary would play imaginary games for hours forgetting to go home for their tea or let Dad know where they had gone. Ioan's father was struggling and found Ioan's forgetfulness an added strain; he blamed Ioan for making life even more difficult, instead of being a helpful boy.

In better times, his father would have understood that Ioan was still a young boy and worried and a bit scared about whether his mother would get better. Dad was so preoccupied now, that he was not someone who Ioan could talk to. Ioan could see that Dad had more than enough on his mind. Ioan's dad wondered why his son didn't try harder, like his big brother David, who helped out by vacuuming the house, or fetching the shopping. It was hard to ask Ioan too, as he was never at home unless it was to sleep. So when Mum started to recover, everyone was greatly relieved and then very surprised when Ioan began to be very irritable and disliked being at home. He would not agree to take showers or brush his teeth like everyone else, and he complained about the cooking and started to be very fussy about the meals his parents prepared. His teacher at school had no concerns, finding him a bright, dedicated pupil who enjoyed the lessons. Arguments began to be more frequent between Ioan and his parents. They wondered if he was turning into a difficult adolescent already. Eventually his grandmother suggested that he come to spend some evenings with her.

Although old and quite frail, Ioan's grandmother enjoyed cooking and kept active doing small amounts of sewing for her neighbours. She had plenty of time on her hands and Ioan had always enjoyed the slow uncritical response of his grandmother. Now she provided the neutralizing influence that he and his parents needed. By spending time with her, Ioan had a break from the pressure at home, and felt that his grandmother could offer an open listening response as she had both time and the gap of a generation. Ioan's parents also had a break from the round of arguments and were pleased that Ioan could talk to his grandmother.

Branching out

Of course, parents do not always feel grateful or glad when relatives offer help and parents have to deal with complicated feelings when their children begin to value the contact with other adults perhaps more than they seem to want parents' time and attention. Despite their better nature, parents might feel rather jealous of a daughter's closeness to her friend's mother or her sudden enthusiasm for swimming with her aunt, when she has always hated her parents' efforts to involve her in similar activities. This development is a forerunner of the later more evident movement away from close family that is an important transition for young teenagers. Many 10- and 11-year-olds will want to try out the experience of different relationships in this way, often seeking reassurance that their home and family is no worse than others. But this can take an uncomfortable form.

Sarah's friend Alezia liked to come to her house after school and together they watched television and ate the chocolate biscuits generously provided by Sarah's mother. When Sarah's mother arrived home from work she was happy to find her daughter and her friend together and encouraged Alezia's curiosity and enjoyment of their comfortable home and lifestyle. She knew that Alezia lived with only her father and older brother and missed out on some of the comforts of having a mother around. She felt it was good for Sarah, too, to find out about a life that was not so easy as her own. Alezia in her turn became attached to the whole family, but especially Sarah's mother. Sometimes she would stay on for a meal with the family, her father grateful that one child was safely looked after.

For Sarah, however, and later Alezia's father, the feelings became more mixed. It was hard for Sarah's mother to understand that Sarah was beginning to feel squashed by Alezia's presence at home. When Sarah tried to say this to her mother, her mother laughed in mock horror, pointing out Sarah's good fortune and insensitivity to Alezia's situation. Similarly, Alezia's father began to feel he might lose Alezia to Sarah's family for good, as she was spending more and more time with them and he began to wonder what kind of woman Sarah's mother could be that she encouraged Alezia to ignore her father and brother. It needed a long conversation between the two parents for the complicated feelings to be sorted out, and for Alezia, Sarah and the adults to see that while Alezia could benefit from her attachment to another family, it was important for the adults to take account of everyone else's feelings too.

Children's perception of their relatives will be informed by their parents' outlook. Our own early years with parents, grandparents and other family members will colour our feelings about their relationships with our children. If there have been difficulties among relatives in the past, arguments with siblings and so on, their input may not be so welcome. It can be helpful to keep in mind that these views will inevitably affect children's perceptions of these individuals. By the age of 10 or 11, children can find great enjoyment and reassurance in relationships with cousins whether or not they have brothers and sisters. A shy, quiet child may be able to explore play and social relationships with cousins who are a little more distant than siblings, yet will have a degree of family cohesion and loyalty that cannot be found among a big class group at school. More confident children will use the contact with cousins as an opportunity to flex emotional muscles. That is, they can more safely explore a sense of themselves and test out their strengths and weaknesses in relationship to their age group. Rivalries and jealousies will also appear just as they do between siblings, but for many children this is tempered by the knowledge that ultimately you have a different origin and different identity from your cousins.

If the relationship between the adults is complicated or strained, then it will be hard for the children in a family to feel free to relate openly. It is not only a matter of relating happily. An enriching relationship is one in which we feel free to express our happiness and agreement, or sadness or anger. At the age of 10 and 11, children will have formed an approach to relationships that will shape their sociability throughout their lives.

It can be useful to remember that by 11, children not only have minds of their own, but also have increasingly a capacity to make more abstract, moral judgements and to work out their own view of the world. This comes as a reminder of their essential separateness, and though there can be great pleasure and comfort in sharing an outlook with your child, he or she may have a relationship with relatives that has a completely different quality from our own contact with the same person. We may struggle to tolerate the views or habits of a sibling who is nevertheless seen as a beloved uncle by our child, but encouraging 10- and 11-year-olds to maintain communication with family members will allow them to gain confidence in their place within the family, and later the wider world.

2

Changing Families: Bereavements, Separations and Dislocations

Coping with changes

It is not uncommon for children to experience a reshuffling of family members during their growing years, as separation and divorce are no longer extraordinary events. This chapter explores the responses of children to family upheavals and radical change, as occur with bereavement, sudden emigration, family breakdown or illness. Perhaps the most devastating and shocking event in any family is the death of a loved one. Studies have shown that our response to this kind of severance can be profound and long lasting. Despite our familiarity with the concept of mortality and the frequent reminders in evidence before us, we are rarely well equipped for the initial impact, or the impact on our children. We now understand from more recent studies and research that children may respond in a variety of ways to a sudden change of this kind and they will manage according to their personalities, and according to their interpretation of the reactions of adults around them. In thinking about the impact of bereavement, we can equally consider the effects of similar large changes, like divorce, or the exodus from a home country in troubling circumstances. In each of these changes, the adults concerned will be trying to find their own equilibrium and may feel stressed by the loss of familiar environments and people.

It would be simplistic and misleading to say that most children will be negatively affected by family breakdown, or likewise to suggest that most children will be relatively resilient, because the breakdown of a family unit or the loss of the prevailing way of life is unsettling for everyone. However, we can consider the potential concerns for children in this age group.

First moments

The moment of a family breakdown, whether parents separating or the termination of a relationship between two adult carers, is a critical time for the adults concerned. It can be almost overwhelming trying to think beyond the painful impact of decisions to end a relationship with all the associated practical and emotional issues, to consider how to help children with this transition. A large change in our lives is not likely to disturb us for only a brief moment, even if the initial shift occurs without warning. Like bereavement, the adjustment following a less complete loss or separation will stretch out over a prolonged time period in which adults and children need to adjust and come to terms slowly with the emotional impact of the change. As we know from the accounts of bereaved people, the process of mourning can be characterized by several chapters of feelings and behaviours, all contributing to the eventual acceptance of our loss. The separation of a couple creates at least discomfort for the two, even if the event is the culmination of mutual discussion and agreement. Often the feelings are sharper: rage, disbelief, jealousy, envy, grief, loneliness and so on. It is not inevitable that children will experience the event with the same degree of feeling, more or less. The most significant part for the children concerned is their parents' or carers' capacities to make room in their minds that can be open to the children's feelings. This can be a huge demand at a time when one may be feeling vulnerable and uncertain oneself.

Families who have established good communications before will probably be able to talk sensitively to children about marital breakdown or the death of an adult or grandparent. It is not essential to deliver absolutely every detail in the service of honesty, as this would not be relevant to the children concerned. A mature 11-year-old may be curious but will not benefit from a discussion with her mother about an unsatisfactory partner, though in general terms it helps to give children of this age as much factual information as possible.

Bryony's parents had been going through a very unsettled patch after her father started to work overseas. Her mother did not want to leave their home town and remove Bryony from her school and make a full-time life abroad, as her husband suggested. Arguments followed and Bryony watched her parents becoming more and more hostile to one another, both feeling misunderstood. Bryony's mother decided to ask her husband to leave and, feeling lonely, she confided in Bryony about her misery and feelings of rejection.

For some months, Bryony did not see her father at all and took some comfort in the closeness of her mother, feeling that she would be able to look after her mother at least. She felt her mother's sadness and the financial worries were proof that her mother was now much too fragile to be bothered with Bryony's ordinary worries about homework or friends. She felt guilty about these concerns and sure that she needed to protect her mother by concealing her own sadness and anger about her parents' separation, and her loss of her father. Eventually, her father returned to their home town and contacted his wife and daughter in the hope of reconciliation for them all. Bryony's parents were able to sort out their difficulties partly through good fortune, as her father was offered a new job nearer home.

Crucially, they were able to keep hold of memories of a good rela-tionship in the past, and overcome their recent conflicts. Things slowly improved much to Bryony's relief, and her parents eventually settled down together again. Even so, Bryony continued to feel anxious for much of her teenage years, feeling that perhaps her parents were very vulnerable, and remained together only because of her.

Paving the way

Once parents decide to part, it is important that children of 10 and 11 are given a clear account of the arrangements and the provision for the future. Often if they feel confident that they are being treated honestly and directly, children will manage their sadness and hurt about the breakdown with distress and interruption to their confidence for a while, before finding their feet once more. Fearing the impact on their children's sense of security and fearing criticism, parents often delay telling children about a separation or plans for the future for as long as possible. The disadvantage for a child is that they can interpret this behaviour on the part of parents as a sign that they have not been considered, and that their feelings of hurt and anger are simply irrel-evant to their parents. Sadly, it is most usually exactly the reverse.

Separations may also include a new family constellation, whether just the fact of mother and father living in separate locations or the addition of a new partner for one or both parents. Sometimes, a new partner will have a family of their own, and so the process of facing the loss of one family, the shift, and the addition of new family members will inevitably be stressful for children. Children may feel doubtful about whether their sadness about their old family, and missing a parent, can be an acceptable subject for their new family.

However, stressful need not mean overwhelming. At this age, a child may appear to take the news quite calmly. Unlike a small child who will be subject to intense, immediate feelings and probably show some aspect of their distress, a 10-year-old may take on the news and display a detachment or quietness. Without doubt, being able to express what you feel can help to find some ease at times of crisis, but attempts to talk to children or to ask them if they would like to talk about their feelings can backfire if they are offered too early on. Some children will find solace in the relationship they have with one or both parents, but others will need to distance themselves and find activities that take their minds away from the difficult real-life issues.

> Saeed was mortified when he realized that his parents had made a plan to separate. His father told him that his mother had returned to her home country for a holiday and to see her relatives. It was only after three or four months, punctuated by two short phone calls from her, that Saeed realized that she was never coming home. When he challenged his father he felt even more angry and distressed on discovering that his parents had discussed this separation and shared a decision not to tell him before his mother left. Saeed had been brought up to put aside expressions of strong feeling and to imitate the polite, careful behaviour of grown men in his family. He was not free to cry and shout as he would like, and managed his painful sense of abandonment by staying away from home as much as possible, keeping himself busy on the library computer at school. He did very well with his end of year project and won the praise of his English teacher, but his quiet, closed manner intensified, and his efforts to channel painful feelings elsewhere exhausted him.

Children may appear almost unable to display any feeling about painful family changes, but as this example indicates, they are not untouched or indifferent to the changes taking place. Rather, the impact can be experienced as something that strikes them practically thoughtless and speechless. It may be necessary to repeat the details of future plans or arrangements to them, or merely to be available in a reliable and predictable routine for a while. With time, children will start to let you know how they are feeling, although it may not take the form of words. It takes courage to look and listen out for the communications your child can give you if you are under strain yourself.

Familiarity and security

Children will usually find the most difficult part of this process comes in the form of a change in their parents. Losses cause pain and bewilderment to adults, and even in the most amicable and carefully planned separations there will be a degree of sadness and preoccupation. Often the separation will represent a period of calm after some time of emotional upheaval and stress, where there have been arguments or dramatic events in the past. In the case of bereavement, death may follow a prolonged chapter of distressing visits to hospital, or the pain of witnessing the deteriorating health of a much loved parent. So at first children may also feel relieved, but will experience the shift in their parents' mood and behaviour as disorienting and unfamiliar. A 10-year-old may face a confusing double loss for a while. The previous world they have known, with its routines and habits, is lost and replaced by a new era with different adults perhaps, but also at times of crisis, the previous mother, father or carer disappears emotionally speaking, no longer available as the same familiar predictable adult the child expected to fall back on. Families, in times of crisis, offer help to parents and this can be a wonderful support. However, at times of stress or breakdown, a child will have complicated feelings of guilt and doubt about what part they might have played in the unfolding break or loss. Above all, the child will feel that almost everything previously known has disappeared, and rather like a fairground mirror, old familiar relationships and faces look different. In the weeks or months of adjustment children need the support of an understanding adult who can provide a consistent experience for them. Grandparents, family friends or teachers can be tremendously helpful to a child.

Despite the temptation to offer children a break from the stress and sadness in the form of a holiday with a relative, these sorties away from home are likely to stir up greater insecurity and concern in the child, even at this later age. This is not a good moment to plan to move house, or visit distant but unfamiliar relatives. Some young children will throw tantrums and become clingy and sleepless if they are anxious, and so too can an older child.

Sometimes parents interpret this behaviour as an expression of criticism or anger and it may be the case, but more usually the irritability and rude behaviour are signs of a child's sense of helplessness, frustration and even depression. So the more the routines of the week and usual locations can be preserved during the acute phase, the more the child can restore a sense of certainty in a climate that is probably confusing and unfamiliar.

Finding courage

Just as parental separations or bereavement stir up strong confusing feelings in children, so too can other major changes within the family group. This may be chronic illness, or a transition to a new home far from the familiar places and people. These changes unsettle all of us and no less children who do not have the benefit of longer experience, as adults do. A child may experience even quite ordinary changes such as a change of school, or the arrival of a grandparent to live with the family, as a worrying sign of permanent change for the worse. Alternatively, another child may manage shifts and changes with relative equanimity and adapt quickly. There is a popular view that children are more flexible and adapt more quickly to changes than we do as adults. Sometimes this is indeed the case, but individuals have their unique view of the world and our responses to new situations will be similarly individual.

Children in this age group may respond quietly to news of marital breakdown or separation, and they will not necessarily display clear signs of grief or anger in response to other kinds of loss. As a parent or carer it will be a delicate balance to find between offering support and attention to their concerns or communications, yet allowing them to distance themselves from troubles at home. There can be a great relief to be found in spending time with friends or being active at school during times of family crisis. On the other hand, a child of this age may find it harder to manage the complicated feelings about his relationship to parents and carers when there are signs of adults feeling vulnerable. This aspect is discussed further in the next chapter.

3

Social Life

Friends and enemies

Many 10- and 11-year-old children have a small group of friends who have been around for a few years. Relationships may start from family contact with neighbours or family friends, but around seven or eight years of age, children more evidently make choices about the kind of companion they favour. This will often arise from a shared interest coupled with a desire to form a kind of strong group with whom to identify. A sense of strength and belonging is especially meaningful for children in the earlier years, as it offers a protection from the unpalatable truth that they are not yet able to have much control over their environment. For some children friendships come easily and are a matter hardly considered by themselves or their carers. Equally there are large numbers of boys and girls who may manage the appearance of friendships but actually struggle to make and keep friends.

As with the wider family, friendships have a significant contribution to the development of the 10- and 11-year-old. The growing consciousness of the real world and the approach of more demands at school will be met with equanimity if we feel surrounded by caring adults and sympathetic friends. Often there are additional difficulties leading to feelings of unease and uncertainty about a capacity to cope with more adult life. By the age of 10 some children will have been trying to cope with doubts and worries about friendships for quite a while. Physical growth for boys and sometimes pubertal changes for girls mark the advent of bigger change. Although most boys will not have any signs of puberty, they will be conscious of their size relative to younger children and older adolescents. Much becomes invested in physical strength for boys, representing both a conventional idea of general masculinity, and contained within that, less conscious concerns about sexual maturity and their potential to become adult men.

Both 10- and 11-year-olds will have extensive experience of relating to other children and at this stage of their lives, friendships will play an important parallel role to family life. Many children also have siblings and will welcome the alternative contact with children outside the family circle. As at an earlier age, friendships have a different meaning and different place in the lives of boys or girls. Whereas girls will probably cultivate a mixture of a few very close friends and a wider group of friends with whom they share activities, boys are more likely to have a small group of friends around specific activities.

Most children will attach themselves to a group during their first years at school, and will have established a social life which can involve playing at one another's homes, or going out to sports or other activities. The social expectations may have been felt quite forcefully, with an element of competition seeping into many social events such as birthday parties or holiday invitations. Despite belonging to a wider group, some children will have already found a small club of close friends.

Best friends

For girls, friendships will be an essential stepping stone in their emotional and social growth. Just like younger girls, 10- and 11-year-olds will be steeped in the culture of the best friend. Most girls and women will form a close friendship that endures through much of their lives, but at this time, the best friend represents a vital transition between the emotional world of the child, and that of the later adult. Before the dawn of adolescence and a more overt preoccupation with romantic attachments and sexual relationships, girls will begin to explore the nature of relationships through their close friendships. Although a friend may become close as a result of a shared experience, whether a passion for a television programme, or a hatred of the science teacher, the external concern or activity will probably be a vehicle for an extensive emotional connection.

Linda and her friend Nell became best friends on the day Linda was sick at school. Her teacher took her to the school nurse to lie down and when she arrived she found her classmate Nell lying on the bench looking pale and floppy. Nell was waiting to go home as she had a temperature and felt sick too. The nurse was busy and clearly flustered by having to find space for two sick students. Both girls talked about their embarrassment and shame at being sick at school and their misery at the hands of the nurse. They discovered that they lived close to one another.

Back at school, and healthy once more, they had a bond arising from their shared experience. For a few weeks, they would chat together at lunchtime, and soon became good friends. Linda enjoyed being able to talk to Nell about things at home or school that she would not want to share with her older sister, who would tease her, or her mother. She and Nell also shared a secret ambition to write a successful novel. When the school holiday came, Nell invited Linda to stay with her family at their seaside cottage for a week. Linda and Nell spent all the time every day sitting on the sofa with pens and exercise books writing their novel, much to the amusement of the rest of Nell's family. At night they would sit up in bed chatting for hours about their writing, their secret hopes, and their views on the world around them. Nell's mum had to persuade them to go outside in the sunny weather.

For Nell and Linda, the discovery of a close relationship provided a chance to experiment in a measured way, to find out not only about themselves, but also how they could negotiate their feelings in exchange with someone else. The intensity would not be available from other family members, and yet it does not involve the complexity of an adult couple's emotional interactions. Many girls find reassurance and confidence as a consequence of the closeness of a best friend.

Unlike the games and occupations of slightly younger girls, at 11, girls will want friendships that are governed by a kind of exclusivity, or even secrecy. In other words, their friendships are probably less concerned with building a sense of confidence about themselves in the wider world and more concerned with finding an experience that reinforces and confirms their growing sense of themselves.

Hannah and her best friend spent every Saturday morning at the shops near their home. Their parents were amused and sometimes frustrated by the routine commitment of the two girls. Taking their pocket money, they liked to go on their own to the local bookshop and the gift shop and spend long periods of time discussing their purchases. But Hannah's parents appreciated that this ritual provided the girls with a valuable independence. Not yet adult enough to go out alone for the day, or to travel unsupervised into the city, they could try out their growing capacity to find their way around, to manage money, and to sample the life of a teenager: looking at clothes, admiring the latest fashionable shoes and dreaming of what they would do if it was their turn to go out to a party. To the spectator, girls of this age have oddly mixed interests. Usually aware of teenage culture that surrounds them, they shun the games and toys of their earlier years and prefer to scan the cosmetic counters or the displays of hair ornaments at the shops. And yet they will also long for sweets and a trip to a children's film.

Best friends are tightly bound together, sometimes against the world outside. On occasions this can be a disadvantage for the girls themselves, when it arises out of a need to establish a small exclusive group. Sometimes, the closeness can be detrimental to others. Nearly all children will indulge in a degree of covert hostility towards other children at some stage. Often this comes into view for a parent or carer when one's own child finds herself victim of her best friend's sudden preference for another girl in class. For a while the new couple are inseparable and the third is left feeling lost and lonely. It can be painful to witness and just as at an earlier age, this behaviour may be a transitory experiment or part of a deeper insecurity on the part of one of the children.

More complex still is the nature of a girl's behaviour towards her friends. Without resorting to bullying or overtly unkind behaviour, many girls lean towards complicated comments and arrangements that both establish the bond with a close friend while simultaneously excluding others. This behaviour can also be seen among boys, who often channel these feelings into behaviour that is governed by formal rules, such as the rules of a club or sporting activity. However, for most children this aspect is an ordinary part of developing a sense of belonging. That is to say, under pressure, they create a closed relationship which cheers and supports them, leaving another child to cope with the discomfort of loneliness.

Some children do not find social relationships easy. If this is the case, it will already have become evident by the time children reach this age. By 10 or 11, children who are struggling to feel comfortable socially will need a great deal of support. Parents and carers can help in a number of ways, including at times some carefully considered engineering. As mentioned already in connection with adapting to changes in school and home life, knowing your child and recognizing his or her personality and qualities can be a great support to your child.

Boys

At this age, many boys have a few closer friends with whom they share active interests. Unlike girls, they may favour interests that involve them in physical action, or they may enjoy pastimes that involve elements of group identity and membership. It is common for children in this age group and younger to evolve complicated imaginary games which require rites and rituals as part of their intention. Children may involve themselves in games that partially allow them to exclude the larger adult world and create a parallel world of their own, and one dimly grasped by adults. Peer group prestige and status are attached to details of acquisition or skill. This tendency is reflected in their enjoyment of games with rules and a structure as well as an imaginative or reasoning aspect. This is clearly the appeal of old favourites such as *Monopoly* and card games, as well as the more contemporary video games and computer games.

Girls

Girls are equally drawn to games and friendships that are bound by a degree of ritual. Some 10-year-old girls may be moving on from games and stories and starting to seek out contact with the culture of older children. If there is a noticeable difference in the quality of girls' friendships it can be seen in the mode of exchange. Even at a younger age, girls will tend to use language as a more immediate channel of contact and communication. Their friendships may well revolve around games or shared swimming lessons at the local pool, but the emphasis is likely to be less on the activity itself, as on an equal amount of discussion, planning, comparing and checking through conversation. This is a general description and there are naturally exceptions to this distinction.

The melting pot: friendship problems

Returning to the matter of loneliness and friendship difficulties, one might wonder how to begin to help boys or girls who do not seem successful in making friends. While most children no longer rely on their parents to make social arrangements with their friends, and seem to start their own round of socializing, the child who cannot do this perhaps feels more isolated than before. In these years, finding oneself not too different from one's peer group is terribly important to children. They are too old now to blithely accept the social engineering of their parents and have an acute sense of any element that might lead to them being perceived as somehow different, let alone odd.

> Belinda was a girl like this. Since her first days at school, she had not found friendships easy. Small and shy, with only a much older sister at home, she found the other children quite imposing at school. Her class had a large number of boys and so the group of girls to choose from was limited. Belinda did not find a kindred spirit in the first years, preferring to watch television on her own at home, or practise tennis at which she excelled. Feeling somewhat isolated she retreated more and more into reading, which she loved and found very easy. While other children played in the playground, she preferred to take her book and daydream about the adventures in the stories. Other children were impressed by her skill but unsure how to invite her to join in. Without the help of an adult to bridge the gap, Belinda and the other children were becoming more segregated. Belinda was intelligent, at ease with maths and science as well as reading, which singled her out further.
>
> At home, Belinda enjoyed listening to her parents and her older sister talking and learned a great deal from sitting quietly reading while they talked. Unfortunately with the passing of time, Belinda began to feel more and more doubtful about how she could get along with the other children at school. She felt embarrassed and lacked confidence about starting to play skipping or join in with collecting charms for a bracelet with the other girls. She did not want them to know how shy and inadequate she felt and disguised this with vivid stories conjured up from her advanced diet of reading. Her teacher was an imaginative person who spotted Belinda's isolation. In the final year of her primary school her teacher suggested that 10-year-old Belinda could take a leading role in the school play. To everyone's surprise Belinda threw herself into her part, which involved a dance sequence and a song, and allowed her to come to life as an entirely different person. This did not solve her problems overnight, but it broke the spell in which Belinda felt she could never make friends with the other girls in her class, and they on their side could see that she was not only a serious girl.

Boys may appear to worry less about friendships, perhaps because they are not so susceptible to the emotional pressure that girls associate with acceptance, whether in family or in the wider circles. However, while boys may seem comfortable enough to continue the patterns of the previous years, playing computer games on their own or practising baseball shots in the park and probably not talking about the nature of friendships, boys are often also troubled by fears of not being accepted by a group. Sometimes, like Belinda, their personality and their home culture makes contact with peers tricky, but when there are worries in the family or difficulties at home, boys may set great store by membership of a group.

As the story of Belinda illustrates, it can happen that a child becomes the subject of unfriendly behaviour and exclusion from friendships. This usually arises from a combination of factors. As children feel very sensitive about their place in social and working groups and worry about vulnerability, they set great significance on belonging and being acceptable to others. This can be advantageous, especially for teachers who can harness the willingness to conform and to work towards a shared goal. But it can stem from an outlook which can be rather rigid and anxiously censorious about any aspect that does not fit in with their picture of the world. Children who feel they are vulnerable will often cope with these feelings by turning their attention to others, who might conceivably be even less of a perfect fit than themselves. At its most extreme this takes the form of overt bullying, but more frequently and insidiously, children will propagate another's doubts through comments and choices of games or playmates. We are all familiar with the powerful attraction of the popular colleague in the office or workplace.

Bullying

It is rare for a child to reach maturity without ever having encountered some tricky patches with their friends or siblings. Many adults will be able to recall episodes of unhappiness during their school years, in which they felt vulnerable and lonely and without the support of friends or adults. Some will say they were bullied, others prefer to normalize the exchanges of aggressive language and behaviour within their peer group. There has been a growing awareness of the prevalence of bullying in its many forms and consequently many educational institutions have forged behaviour guidelines and written policies to tackle bullying. Even this vocabulary use here echoes the intentions of concerned adults, to demonstrate their strength and size in overpowering any aggressive or cruel behaviour. Naturally parents and children want to be assured that schools are thinking and acting to protect the vulnerable members of the groups. A clear policy that has the support and commitment of all the adults in a school can be very effective in dealing with incidents.

Children of 10 and 11 will already have evolved fairly complex approaches to managing relationships with others, and will usually have an extensive experience of the frustrations and pains, as well as the delights, that are characteristic of any close relationships. One would expect that in early years children have struggled to manage strong feelings and found a battery of ways of protecting themselves in the face of disappointments or disagreements or failures. For example, children of 8, 9 and 10 will naturally tend to seek out games and exchanges that structure and moderate the distress that raw feelings might otherwise cause.

> While competing with an anonymous other on his video game or collecting bubblegum cards, Gary had a sense of order and routine which was much more comfortable than the painful feelings of helplessness he experienced in the face of his big brother's friends teasing him with invitations to race them on his bike. Gary found satisfaction and relief from being able to measure the gap between the number of cards he already had and the full set. He knew that in time, he could bask in the status of being the first boy to collect the whole set.

Children of 10 enjoy games and activities that might seem somewhat dull and inflexible to their parents, or to older children. The insistence on order and membership, and an enjoyment of establishing groups at the expense of thinking about individual characteristics, will have dominated. But now, there is a gradual dawning of a more subtle and complex idea of friendships and sharing. All being well, a broader, more open interest in others can now develop alongside a growing awareness of adolescence. Children can continue to be quite preoccupied with conventions and group membership leading to the potential for bullying, or becoming bullied.

Feeling like Cinderella

> Zahara is a 10-year-old girl who moved to Europe with her family two years ago. Her father had a prestigious professional post in his home country, and was able to keep his family in a luxurious lifestyle. His daughters were used to living in a large house with staff to care for them, and a private car to drive them around town. A change in the political climate meant that Zahara's father decided hastily to leave his country and take his family to a safer environment. The family had no difficulty finding a home and settling into western European life, but

Zahara found the move difficult. As the youngest girl she had often wondered whether her bigger sister and her mother noticed her. She longed for a regular period of time with her father, but he was always busy working. The family's privileged life in their home country had often caused the girls to be quite isolated from other children. None of this had mattered until they moved. Zahara had already found that she could get along better if she occupied herself with all the toys and pretty clothes in her bedroom. Her parents reminded her often of her advantages and said she should be grateful. She was, and she felt quite triumphant and strong when she sat next to the other girls in class. "Don't you have a proper pencil sharpener?" she asked her neighbour, airily waving her special Disneyland Mickey Mouse pencil sharpener in front of her companion.

Once in Europe, Zahara felt all the certainty and the benefit of her superior position at school had vanished. Suddenly she and her family had no special position and Zahara had to join a class of girls who had been together since nursery school. Finding herself an outsider and feeling rather like Cinderella after the clock has struck midnight, Zahara instinctively turned to a way of coping that had been very soothing in the past. Without a thought she soon identified the girl in the class who, like her, did not seem to fit in so easily. Lizzie was a tall, thin girl who did not like playing physical games at playtime and seemed rather timid when it came to the sports activities. Zahara felt immediately better in her new class realizing that however different she was, Lizzie could be relied upon to stick out even more.

Before long Zahara had made a bid to become the best friend of Tacey, who had the longest hair and the neatest hand writing and who always brought her lunch from home, packed in a special fashionable lunch box. As they ran out to the playground after lunch, Zahara called out to Lizzie in light tones, "Come on! Can't you run faster than that!" Later she sidled up to Lizzie and asked her quietly why she bothered coming out to the playground because everyone would laugh at her hopping about like a stork with skinny legs.

When Lizzie eventually told her teacher about Zahara's unkind remarks, the teacher scolded Zahara and suggested she tried to make friends with everyone in class. But for Zahara, it was impossible to feel safe and confident and to enjoy the more open, flexible atmosphere of the class of 10- and 11-year-olds. Eventually her mother was summoned to school. She was distressed to think that her daughter could ever be a bully, especially as she was so quiet at home and idolized her big sister. Zahara's mother wondered if her daughter was being picked on as she was evidently from another culture.

The soft underbelly

Bullying is distressing and isolating for the victim, particularly as the details often sound relatively mild when relayed to adults. Whether physical or verbal cruelty, girls are often able to spin subtle, veiled threats to others, making the bullying much harder to identify and deal with. Boys too may find words to wound their peers and siblings, though they are more likely to resort to direct threats of physical violence. Coupled with the tendency of children in these years to feel a tremendous sense of loyalty and a commitment to structures, there can be great confusion about who can be told, who can be included in information. There are occasional tragedies when children feel completely isolated and unable to imagine sharing their misery with an adult, and as parents and carers we identify with our children, and wish to protect them from suffering. So it can be difficult to encourage children to regard their feelings of vulnerability as a universal and tolerable aspect of being human. But bullying is more likely among children who are unsure of who can help them with the difficult feelings of being small, incompetent or jealous, to name just a few of the feelings.

As the story of Zahara indicates, bullies are not usually the biggest or noisiest members of the group. More often they are the children who have in some sense suffered themselves. From an outsider's perspective this can be hard to spot, and we are familiar with the bullies of children's fiction, such as Draco Malfoy in the Harry Potter stories by J.K. Rowling, the Snow Queen in the *Narnia Chronicles* (C.S. Lewis), or Flashman in *Tom Brown's Schooldays* (Thomas Hughes). Children who are particularly anxious about belonging, finding a secure space for themselves in their families, or feeling overlooked, can become especially attracted to the notion of insiders and outsiders. It is harder for them to imagine a mixed group with an appreciation of all kinds of individuality. This is not the developmental era in which eccentricity or stark individuality is appreciated, but by 10 and 11, some children will be able to tolerate and even enjoy contact with individuals who in one way or another could be culturally different from themselves.

It is thin support for the victim of bullying to remind them of the emptiness or evident absurdity of the bully's remarks. It may not be immediately helpful, to encourage the victim to find a tougher persona. In the first instance the victim of bullying needs to see that concern and understanding is applied to both the bully and the victim, but that bullying meets with a decisive punishment.

Recognizing signs of unhappiness

Coping with bullying will largely depend on confidence. A 10- or 11-year-old who feels able to communicate, and who feels a sense of worth and belonging, should be able to shake off bullying in whatever form. It is the children who for one reason or another feel less sure of themselves, who may first attract the attention of children who are troubled and exercise their physical or emotional strength on others, and these are the children less likely to seek out help or feel able to alert adults to any malicious behaviour they encounter. So how can one help less confident children to manage the climate of school life and to enjoy contact with their peers?

It is the boys and girls who have been encouraged to talk about their outlook and their feelings who become confident and at ease in the company of others. Naturally, in families who feel more comfortable about sharing their emotional responses, and who regularly share conversations, there will be a sturdy sense of belonging in the children's minds. Despite difficulties in a family such as those already described, many children will feel confident about finding a supportive, listening ear where there has been experience of talking and thinking together. This can also help a child to keep hold of an idea of caring supportive adults even at times when the reality is somewhat different, and they are more likely to seek out this kind of response from adults.

Friendly resilience: the benefit of optimism

When Donny started at a traditional English school after the relaxed atmosphere of his American junior school, he was surprised and annoyed to be treated with impersonal, careless detachment by the teachers. When some of the older boys began to tease him about his accent and his haircut, Donny immediately reported their jibes to his form teacher, only to meet with an uninterested comment. For a day or two Donny was utterly miserable, feeling shocked and let down by the teachers, and excluded from the English culture he would never belong to. Soon his disappointment turned to anger, and he went back to school and tried again to talk to his form teacher. It took persistence and a certain confidence for Donny to insist that his form teacher listen to his concerns, but because he was used to talking to his parents, his teachers and the other adults in the small community of his home town, he was not deterred by the cool reception he first received.

4

Changing Body Changing Self

Physical developments

Perhaps at no other age are the physical variations between children so notice-able. Looking at a group of 10- and 11-year-olds, one immediately sees a huge range of heights, shapes and sizes. Like other aspects of development, physical and sexual maturity begins at different times for each child, and so a room of 10-year-olds will no doubt include one or two small, slender boys, perhaps a tall, well-built imposing boy, and several who already show the characteristic gangliness of the young teenager. The girls among them will be equally assorted. Some will be tall and boyish while others remain quite petite, others again already at puberty. The bodily changes in girls are more evident and usually appear earlier than their male contemporaries.

By the age of 10 most girls will have the beginning of the curved body shape of the adult woman and have developing breasts. Some will also have started menstruating. As the onset of puberty is earlier, the relationship between boys and girls has inevitably altered from previous generations. Girls and boys will already have established an identity with their gender, probably preferring the company of their own sex as playmates or companions. They will have formed relationships with others who become close allies with whom to share not only activities, but dreams and ambitions. The evidence of their bodies changing can be quite disconcerting for girls at this time. It is not simply the dawning of menstruation and its accompanying association with an adult life of sexual relationships and parenting, but the evidence of a well-known way of life coming to an end. This can be seen among girls who reach puberty early and who are trying to find a sense of themselves among a peer group who may generally be later developers.

An ugly duckling or a swan?

Charlie found herself in this position. Adopted in her infancy from an eastern European country, she had thrived during her young years. Her parents had always felt at ease talking to her about the adoption, her birth family and their own attachment to her. She was a happy and lively little girl, popular among her classmates for her pretty shiny hair and talent for English and drama. The family had a younger child of their own, who admired her older sister and with whom Charlie could enjoy the pleasure of being older and more accomplished. By the time she was nine, though, Charlie's body began to change. She loved sports of all kinds and was seen as a reliable and enthusiastic member of her class. She was equally at home in drama and musical activities at school.

Quite suddenly she started to feel anxious and to make excuses to miss some of the after-school sports clubs and seemed to isolate herself from the other children. Her mother noticed the marked shift in Charlie and talked to her to try to reassure her about the changes that were taking place in her body. With her first period, Charlie lost much of her confidence, doubting her mother's view that it was normal and a positive sign of her healthy development. It wasn't only the embarrassment of being different from the other girls at school and the worry about how to manage the practical matters of hygiene, but in Charlie's mind, the onset of puberty before most of her peers connected with rumbling worries about her origins. She felt as if this unwelcome change was evidence that she did not really belong, despite her popularity. Paradoxically, some of her close friends viewed her with awe, and she gained an added respect and sympathy from them.

Charlie was impatient: "They don't know what it's like," she shouted at her mother. One can see that for Charlie the early development was quite isolating and she needed considerable reassurance. Luckily her mother had already established a closeness which allowed her to continue to be a listening ear for Charlie. Inevitably perhaps, as Charlie began to feel a bit more at ease in her new body and to put aside fears that she was permanently different from others because she was adopted, she also began to build closer friendships with one or two girls and confided less in her mother. Instead she sought the company of girls who could look forward to membership of a new group: teenagers.

Naturally, girls and boys will turn to their friends and peers but those relationships will be coloured by their earlier relationships with parents, particularly same-sex parents. For Charlie, a difficult transition was greatly assisted by her mother's open attitude and willingness to make space for Charlie's concerns, however unrealistic they seemed to her. This warmth and closeness provided a template in Charlie's mind for the kind of relationship she could have with friends, and later, boys or adult partners.

Some girls will experience the onset of puberty as welcome evidence of their health and ordinariness, but nevertheless feel a sense of loss. Like Charlie, they may feel an anger or even jealousy of other children, with the associations of adult life and sexuality that accompany menstruation. On the whole these worries will subside with reassurance and a growing confidence, but on occasions the emotional impact of increased hormone activity alongside the physical discomforts of period pains can accumulate to create a more persistent withdrawal and lack of self-esteem. Just as older adolescents struggle with worries about their identity and wonder how they will ever transform into adults, 10- and 11-year-olds may suffer a sense of dislocation and loss, unsure if they can still function as a child, being too young for boyfriends and teenage activities, but somehow no longer carefree and interested in the physical games of their younger days.

For girls who are developing at a more average pace, puberty may be quite a way off and yet they too can feel very uncertain. Some girls feel anxious about the prospect of menstruation and they will steadfastly ignore any signs in themselves or others of the inevitable changes taking place both physically and emotionally. This can be seen in 10- and 11-year-old girls who become intensely involved in games and preoccupations that seem young for them.

> Satu felt very troubled by what she had heard about adolescence and also felt little beside some of the girls in her class. She enjoyed watching television and following an internet website that monitored and distributed information about endangered animals in Asia and Africa. Increasingly she preferred to read the books she had read before, returning to the funny stories of her young childhood and wanting to watch films with fairytale themes. Her parents were amused and puzzled by her "old-fashioned" identity. Later, though, she began slowly to emerge and to take an interest in activities and conversations that were more relevant for her age. Satu became more confident and certain about her own development but she had needed to revisit the pleasures and safe familiarity of young childhood before she could be ready to leave it behind and progress to a new physical and emotional era.

Each child will have their own particular anxieties, hopes and expectations of their changing bodies. Some children are accommodated more comfortably by their parents than the teenagers would be in a family. In other families, there is an ease and enjoyment of the dawn of adolescence with opportunities for both parents and children to shift into a new relationship together. Sometimes we recall our own bewilderment or excitement at the development of a "new" body, or our disappointment at being left behind. Our children may share these feelings or actually feel quite differently from us, so there is no checklist for this phase.

Boy wonder

Physical development will largely continue as in the previous three years for boys. It is unlikely that they will be affected by the physical body changes associated with sexual development at 10 and 11, but there are exceptions. They will be conscious of the changes taking place in other children around them, though. On the whole, however, boys in this age group will not face the emotional challenge connected to a physical change as the girls do. However, with an emerging awareness of sexuality and perhaps curiosity and doubts about how a transformation can take place, boys too can be preoccupied by their bodies. Children's play of every kind can be thought of as a research project. Through play they explore and investigate not only the external world, but also their own internal psychological capacities. This is more obvious when we see a toddler who is putting her teddy to bed in her own baby clothes, but can be seen in older children's make-believe games and fascination with science fiction stories and robot toys.

Toys and construction sets are often designed for children to create creatures or objects that transform, grow or access extraordinary capabilities. The manufacturers emphasize the opportunities for imagination and reasoning, but these toys offer valuable research opportunities, working through the possibilities of their own development mentally, emotionally and physically. It may be quite impossible for a small 10-year-old boy to believe that he could ever grow into a muscular, tall and potent adult man, without plenty of time to try out imaginary possibilities.

Similarly, physical games and an awareness of one's body play an important part in a boy's confidence in his own development. Physical exploration of one's own body and its responses are a contribution to an acceptance of later physical and sexual life.

5

School Life

Managing transitions

At around this age children will encounter a shift in their educational life. For many children this is formalized by a change of school, marking the start of a more specific academic life. For others, while they will continue to attend the same school, there will be a move to introduce a more challenging schedule of learning. Teachers and educational programmes will expect an increased capacity for reasoning and independent thinking in response to the provision in the classroom. Sometimes this appears as a development in the form of questions put to children, whether in maths and language lessons, or in other areas such as history, science, geography and so on. Whereas previously children were given a variety of opportunities to approach the learning process, a narrowing begins with less emphasis on play and learning through physical experience, and a tendency to rely on reading, writing and reasoning in its place. Children manage the challenges of remembering facts and they often enjoy the sense of strength and order that a command of information can bring them. Until they reach 10 or later, they are not really ready to think around a subject taking up different perspectives or balancing out contrasting data, but now they can draw on a body of life experiences which contribute to their memory. Our memories store not only details of a factual kind, but also emotional experience which colours and shapes our understanding of the world. With this dynamic accumulation of experience, the 10-year-old can begin to think and reason with more information and experience. This enables them to be more truly empathic, to imagine a world that is different from their own, yet peopled by others who have common feelings. Just as young children recognize the feelings of their mother, so 10-year-olds can recognize the dilemmas and choices facing others and begin to apply their own experience to help them form a point of view.

School work probably also requires children of this age to manage a degree of independent work and organization. An era begins during which the child must learn to cope with remembering which books will be needed for which subjects, carry them from one location to another and probably manage more complex timetable arrangements than earlier. Most 10- and 11-year-olds are quite ready for this increase in responsibility and independence, but as with every other step, children will not always reach the required capacity at the designated age and some find the shift quite hard to accommodate. Again, our children's capacity to manage the new school regime will be partly influenced by our own feelings and experiences of school life.

Sometimes the higher expectation and associated shift in the structure at school is confined to the school day, but most children will also be expected to work at home on a regular basis. Many are helped by having already had a routine that included a small amount of homework, but now a degree of motivation and organization will be required. The advent of more academic study is often felt as a challenge not only to the children themselves, but to parents too. Some boys and girls have an aptitude for reading and enjoy the satisfaction of exploring on their own and will thrive on the challenges set by teachers, looking forward to the complexity of more advanced study.

For those children who will be coming up to a change of school, there is the added challenge of leaving behind a familiar environment, including the familiar faces of teachers and support staff, to join a large senior community where they will be the youngest and smallest members. Unlike primary school, the secondary school will not offer the same attention to individual children, either in terms of their learning or social development. A child may be used to remaining in one classroom for most of the school week, being taught by one or two teachers, with his or her work proudly displayed on the classroom walls by the class teacher. The move to secondary school can be quite shocking, imposing as it does another culture. In these classrooms, it is not the students but the subject which is given pride of place. Students are likely to be asked to take charge of their own books and belongings, storing them in cloakrooms and lockers without the home of a permanent classroom. No longer a member of a group of 20 or 30, the child is plunged into a world in which teachers view him or her as one of many groups of students. Closer to the external adult world of work and responsibility, the life of secondary or high school can be unsettling for a child who is not quite ready for this level of independence.

Key skills

In order to make use of the learning opportunities, to be able to draw on experience and to start to apply one's own ideas and opinions, one must feel relatively confident and comfortable in the world. In particular, this relies on feeling one has the foundation skills to hand: reading, writing and arithmetic. There is much anxiety in all quarters about the success or otherwise of reading and maths programmes and this seems to reflect a divide between ideas of encouraging learning as a source of enjoyment and enrichment, and apparently contrasting ideas about the importance of a directive structure with recognizable rules for students. As a result children may be conscious of prevailing doubts about whether they have banked enough skills and whether they have the raw materials to allow them to think confidently about the world they live in. Most children will have been tested and any difficulties identified, so that extra help with the foundation subjects should be provided to prepare them. Sometimes, however, for a variety of reasons, those skills have not been established and an 11-year-old finds the pressure of the new educational expectations thoroughly intimidating.

A 10- or 11-year-old may have some specific difficulty with learning, such as finding numbers and letters difficult to decode and remember. Others may find they can understand written instructions well, but cannot manage to make sense of information they hear in the classroom. Teachers and psychologists are increasingly aware of these inefficiencies that can be the signs of temporary shifts in the all-round balance of development. It can make the task of reading and arithmetic particularly hard for some children, and extra individually designed support can be provided. Indeed at around this age most teachers will be giving particular attention to this very matter and trying to ensure that the child is fully prepared for the learning ahead. Sometimes parents might feel that teachers are not aware of a difficulty their child is having with learning and this may be because teachers have not been able to gather sufficient information about the child's work to identify a problem in detail. In the early years of a child's school life, it can be valuable for parents to build a relationship with school staff who are more readily available to parents and carers and probably have a fuller knowledge of your child as a whole person. Later, communication with teachers and other staff becomes less immediate, and teachers have less involvement with the individual emotional needs of the students in their classes. It can fall to the dedication of parents and carers to ensure that a channel of communication is kept going. Alerting teachers to a child's difficulties at school can be tremendously helpful to teaching staff. Naturally, some exploration of the possible cause will be needed.

A child may have difficulty with the set reading homework, for example, for a number of reasons. Some difficulties may be a sign of learning struggles and then a careful exploration is needed to decide whether it is a problem that needs remedial educational support or one that is transient and a sign of a temporary delay. It can also happen that difficulties with school work are an indication of a child's other concerns. Children who are worried about life at home, or who have been ill, will find it hard to give their full attention to the details of maths formulae or rainfall comparisons. One can see that it can be quite complex for a good teacher to evaluate the extent of a learning difficulty, and on the whole teachers are grateful for the insight that parents can bring.

Stretching out

The 10- and 11-year-old will be occupying an awkward place within the educational world too. They are being asked to take on a more mature approach not only to learning, but also to independence and responsibility, yet many children will still be needing the containment of a more monitored and guided environment. Often it is not the classroom, but the life outside in the dining hall, or the corridor, or the playground that occurs as the most daunting aspect in the child's mind. Although the new-found independence of unsupervised library time, or sports clubs and societies, can provide youngsters with a great deal of confidence, for some children the freer but less bounded world, mostly within the gaze of their peer group, can be overwhelming.

> Danny was a small but very bright 11-year-old who started at the same secondary school as his brother, who was three years older. Initially a little scared, Danny showed himself to be full of bravado. He strode into the gate every morning calling out to classmates in a loud voice. He held their attention with jokes and tall stories about what he got up to after school. Once in the classroom, he continued to entertain his mates, pulling faces and fidgeting, just as he had done at his primary school. There he had been very successful in getting his teacher's exas-

perated attention and enjoyed huge popularity as the naughty, cheeky boy in his class. Despite his behaviour, his teacher had been able to handle his outbursts and understood that Danny's underlying worry was about being small.

In his new school, though, Danny was regarded with less patience. His buffoonery was seen as time wasting and attention seeking by the teacher who came to take the register. Danny's bids for attention were interpreted as a challenge to the authority of the school structure. The teachers took action in the form of detentions and extra homework to exert their authority. Things might have escalated for Danny, who secretly longed to do as well as his older brother, but a parents' evening during the first term gave his mother an opportunity to share some of her understanding of Danny with school staff. Once she had alerted them to Danny's worry about being the small boy in class and his worry that he would never stand out or be as impressive as his brother, his class teacher felt more sympathy for Danny and made an arrangement for him to have a companion when he went to lunch, or had to travel to the sports field, a bus ride away. This enabled Danny to gain confidence about the new way of life without his anxiety being named and identified by everyone. Instead he quickly felt proud of his association with an older pupil and started to feel more hopeful about managing the school day; only then did he feel ready to tackle the new work presented by his teachers.

Apart from fairly usual worries that we can all remember from our school days, some children experience difficulty with the work or the way of life at school as a consequence of a separate event. For instance, unexpected illness can be very troublesome for children at a point when the demand from school life is quite high.

Mishaps

Candy is a lively 11-year-old girl with lots of friends and many inter-ests, from riding to trampolining at her local leisure centre. During her first month at secondary school, Candy fell off a pony and broke her leg. After the initial shock Candy settled down to the business of being in hospital, as her leg had needed pinning and she had to stay in bed for some weeks. Candy had looked forward to her new school and was very pleased to start with two friends from her previous school. Her parents had been a bit concerned about the journey, which involved quite a long walk and then a bus ride to school, but Candy had taken well to the new regime. The broken leg was a real blow to her, separating her from her old friends and her newly found companions. Her class were sympathetic and the teacher allowed them to use an English lesson to write her cards and stories. Her friends went to visit her in the hospital and Candy's family encouraged them to phone Candy or visit when they wanted. Candy had to miss the rest of the term and in the spring she could only return to school by hobbling on her crutches.

A smiling, outgoing girl, Candy attracted sympathetic interest. Teachers and pupils who had not really known her at the start of the school year had come to know about her and came to enquire after her. She had received some help with school work while in hospital but of course she had missed a great deal. She was worried about whether she could fit in as she had been away for so long and especially worried about French as she had never learnt another language before. In the first weeks she was very tired and irritable, feeling almost overwhelmed by the task of catching up, but with encouragement and the positive remarks of adults, she started to slot back into place. By the time the end of year exams came, Candy managed to do just as well as her friends who had joined with her at the start of the school year.

By contrast, Alex had also looked forward to starting at the new school as she was a fast learner and enjoyed the prospect of tackling more complex work at school and being given more freedom to study in her own time. She also had a friend who travelled to school with her and started at the new school site. Though not bubbly and smiling like Candy, she was liked by students and admired by teachers who identified a committed and thoughtful girl with great potential. She settled calmly into school life, tackling the homework with enthusiasm and often extending the work required. She was also a mature girl supported by a quiet, professional family who valued independent study and thinking.

Sadly, towards Christmas, Alex fell ill and had to take time off school. At first the doctor could not identify her illness and sent her for tests at the local hospital. While waiting for the appointment Alex became more unwell until she was admitted to hospital and found to be suffering from a chronic kidney disease. After her return home, Alex remained quite ill for several months and had to attend hospital regularly. She too had to miss most of her first term at school. The staff prepared work for Alex to do at home and she began to spend her time at home drawing and listening to music. Her friends came to see her at home, but as she was still feeling unwell, she found their visits tiring and also upsetting, as they talked about all the fun they had playing games, joining new clubs and taking part in new school activities.

Alex was keen to get back to school in the new term and felt confident that she could make up the lost work. However, her return to the class was not as easy as hoped. In the weeks she had missed, she had become quieter and more serious during her illness, and the girls in her class had found their feet in the social life of the school. Alex struggled to establish relationships with the other girls, feeling that she was a late additional arrival. Although over the following term she began to recover and earned respect from the others for her diligence and cleverness as well as finding a new friend, she remained somewhat separate and did not regain the confidence she had before her illness. Alex recovered from the blow to her self-esteem slowly, and despite academic success, it was some years before she could feel relaxed and free from anxiety about the idea of illness recurring.

These two girls responded quite differently to an unfortunate event and one can see how the reaction of family and friends, as well as their innate personalities, influenced their response to setbacks.

Other setbacks can appear in the form of family difficulties or concerns.

Home versus school

Marek is a boy who always goes along with his friends. On the whole he is thought of as an easy going, intelligent but not too ambitious boy, who prefers to spend his time with his video games or watching soccer, if he can. Like his friends he had some reservations about what life might be like in secondary school and was pleased when they were taken for a day's visit to the large mixed school. He wondered whether he would cope with the work and how he would remember everything, but he also looked forward to the big sports field and a whole afternoon every week for soccer. During the long summer holiday, Marek and his sister stayed with their aunt, uncle and cousins abroad.

While they were away his parents were in the process of trying to sort out severe financial problems following the collapse of the father's business. Marek's father concluded that they would need to sell the family home and move to a smaller house in order to survive economically. Marek's mother was very upset as she loved the house and had many good friends nearby. Marek and his sister returned to find the packing up in progress and his parents trying bravely to reassure the children. The house had to be sold quickly and as the school term started, the family moved into a rented flat. His parents were worried about the impact on the children and tried to talk to them about the changes. Marek was very angry, blaming his dad for causing them all this unhappiness. His mother in turn was angry with Marek for adding to his father's guilt and anxiety. Marek took comfort from the days at school, glad to be away from the impersonal flat. But despite his earlier enthusiasm and his relief at being among friends, Marek found he could not get down to the work set for him. He muddled on as before, not really causing great concern to teachers or his parents until the end of the year. The exams showed that he had hardly taken in anything of the lessons. His teacher was impatient, and Marek was humiliated by the sudden notoriety he had gained.

It was not obvious to anyone, even Marek himself, that school life could not take his mind off his anxiety about his family. Mum and Dad had recovered well, and though they all had to manage hard times, things were improving and Dad had a new job, so it was puzzling to everyone that Marek's work had fallen behind. His father recognized Marek's relaxed attitude and half-hearted commitment and considered Marek's behaviour to be a sign of his age and something he would grow out of. His mother agreed until his teacher pointed out inconsistencies. Marek was quite able to achieve good marks in physics and maths.

Marek himself felt very uncomfortable about any fuss and for a while everything became tense and even worse as all the adults seemed to be focusing on him, which only made him embarrassed and guilty. It was very difficult to imagine just how anxious he was underneath and how hard he found it to concentrate on the world outside or let himself think about anything much. The demands of English or history lessons were quite overwhelming, requiring him to use his imagination and to piece together subjective details. If Marek let himself think about these kinds of things he might also feel overwhelmed with feelings and memories about his old home and his previous life when he could take safety and security for granted. For Marek the timing of his parents' difficulties overlapped unluckily with his own dawning sense of leaving infancy and a comfortable world behind.

As these examples indicate, there is a degree of pressure on children of this age that can be considered universal and as parents or carers, we may view these years before the teens as being relatively straightforward because they do not involve the intense emotional changes we associate with adolescence. The ease of school transitions will largely depend on the combination of family culture, the child's personality and the expectations of schools and peer group. Parents are still hugely influential in their children's lives, though it may seem less obvious at this point. Parents sometimes find themselves surprised by a sudden leap of development in their children and so it can be hard to judge what kind of support to offer.

A different outlook

Marie's mother had hated secondary school. Being a shy girl without brothers and sisters, she had been terrified by the first days in the enormous playground and the noisy boisterous behaviour of the older students. She wanted to help Marie and protect her from the unpleasantness that Marie might encounter. She talked to Marie a lot about the coming change of school and how she might be prepared for all the challenges ahead. This was very helpful to Marie in some respects, and she enjoyed collecting all the new stationery for the term ahead and buying her new uniform. On the first day, however, she was very nervous so her mother took some time off work and accompanied her to the school gates. Mum waited to make sure Marie was all right and then departed. Marie was quiet at the end of the day and became quieter still as the week progressed. Actually she was relieved to find that it was much more enjoyable than her mother had suggested, but Mum was worried about Marie's quietness and asked to see her class teacher on Friday afternoon. The teacher reported that Marie was settling in well and seemed happy with the other girls. Marie's mother felt the teacher probably did not appreciate how good Marie might be at hiding her anxiety because she wanted to blend into the class group. They agreed to speak about this a week later.

The following week produced a similar response in Marie. Her mother tried to prompt her, asking about the school day, wondering if anything was worrying her. Marie shrugged and said it was all fine. Her teacher too related that Marie appeared to be enjoying her days and was making friends with a couple of other girls who were quieter girls in the group. Eventually Marie's mother had to withdraw, feeling very frustrated and worried, but helpless. She imagined Marie becoming quieter and quieter, falling behind in her work, and probably having to think of leaving school at the earliest opportunity.

It was a surprise, a shock even, when some months later Marie began to talk enthusiastically about starting Spanish, as she was really enjoying the French lessons and looked forward to adding another language. Marie and her friend were the best at languages in their year group, a fact they were very proud of. Marie's mother slowly overcame her surprise and realized that her daughter had inherited other aspects of her parents' personalities. While she had felt anxious and worried about Marie's shyness and imagined she would suffer at school as mother herself had done, Marie was far more at ease and confident than she realized. Marie, in turn, felt very loyal to her mother and had found it hard to share the extent of her pleasure and enjoyment of school.

Although children often do inherit characteristics with their parents, and will most likely mirror some of their traits or talents, they are often very separate from us in other respects. This can be quite confusing for a parent in these years. Later, their wish to assert their own personality and to shape an identity of their own becomes more evident, but during these years parents may have to reassess their role and contribution to their child's development. An ability to develop alongside children will no doubt be shaped by our own childhood experiences.

6

Hard Times: When Help Is Needed

Parents and carers can help children throughout their early years to gain confidence in communicating, rather than acting on their feelings without reflection, partly by establishing and encouraging the communications of their children as part of family life. This is slightly different from encouraging children to fill up and overtake the space that might reasonably be expected to be given to the conversations and interests of adults. Discovering that you have a space in time and the thoughts of your parents and relatives is an asset to a child, but not helpful if it amounts to a feeling that you have a right to take up all the available talking and thinking time in your family.

For many people expressing and articulating their feelings does not come naturally and one may wonder how to foster ease in one's children. Families who are more reserved in their expressions are not necessarily promoting difficulty for children. Turning back to the worry that many parents and carers have, namely how does one know if one's child is struggling alone with anxiety or distress, it is useful to consider what one knows of a child in the previous nine or ten years.

In short, it is difficult to consider a set of criteria to use for assessing possibility of a hidden worry or problem, but keeping a child's outlook in mind and thinking back over past events will be a valuable indicator of change. For example, children who have always been fussy about their food may become more so at times of change or stress, only to return to a fairly predictable pattern once they feel more settled. In another child a sudden loss of appetite might have more significance. While 10- and 11-year-olds have already developed quite extensive mechanisms for coping and may not become so evidently upset as younger children, a sustained change in mood and outlook might be reason to consider whether there are new stresses in the child's environment.

Helping our children to grow

All the descriptions of children so far and the discussion in the book have looked at the ordinary worries of 10- and 11-year-olds and their parents and carers. Sometimes the difficulties are just as ordinary but harder to put right. By this age, some of these problems will already have become evident, for example children who have a delay in their capacity to learn, or children who may have shown signs of difficulty in relating to others, as with autism. So it is less likely that more complex needs will emerge for the first time.

The 10- and 11-year-old will be treading a path between continuing childhood and the brink of adolescence and this can be challenging for some parents. This aside, the child's personality will have a large influence on his or her response to the usual ups and downs of life. For some children, change of country or the loss of a parent will be upsetting and painful, but ultimately they will find their feet again and continue to develop well. Other children have complex, sensitive personalities and find themselves easily knocked off balance. So how can one judge when further help might be needed? If help is needed, is it a sign of a lasting "weakness" or deficiency? This is a time in a child's life when many external factors impinge on him or her and so a patch of anxiety or friendship problems is probably not unusual. But if a child continues to be withdrawn, or easily becomes angry and distressed by contact with adults despite attempts to support or sympathize with them, perhaps an outside perspective can be useful. For example, as discussed in the previous section, a child may be unhappy despite no obvious change in family circumstances or any evidence of difficulties at school. Often trained professionals working with children are not only experts with knowledge, but also people with whom parents can find a shared interest in trying to understand their children, their persistent worries or behavioural patterns.

Special educational needs

There has been a great advance in the appreciation of the specific difficulties some children have in being able to learn, and most schools nowadays will have a designated member of staff whose task is to assess and plan how to help children who have been identified as needing help. However, the educational framework naturally concentrates on how to help a child to access the skills he or she will need in order to read and write, to manage maths, and later to pass examinations. It is recognized that some children are not so able to respond to the approach to learning generally on offer and that the underlying reasons may be complex. A combination, often, of a different perceptual capacity and associated anxieties that quickly arise in response to the demands of classroom learning, usually contribute to a child's lack of concentration or real struggle to remember letters and numbers. Few things conjure up as much anxiety in parents and children as a lack of progress.

As with other aspects of children's development, it is unlikely that a 10- or 11-year-old will have gone unnoticed if he or she has difficulty with school work. Occasionally children are able to exert huge resources and with quick intelligence find ways around their difficulties unaided. If this is the case it is usually the approach of a narrower academic curriculum that first sheds light on the problem.

> Pia had always enjoyed her days at school not only because she was a very sociable little girl but also because she loved stories and had a strong curiosity about everyone and everything. When she and her classmates started to recognize letters and began the first steps in reading, Pia was frustrated because she longed to be able to read properly and to find out what happened in the stories in her reading books. Try as she might she could not keep up with the other girls in her group, but she found that by reading the last sentence in each paragraph she could follow what was going on and even answer the teacher's questions. It was a huge relief to find a good strategy for keeping up; the trouble was that she had to guess the missing bits that she had no time to read through. Until she was in her last year of primary school Pia managed well enough although she was often tired and fretful at the end of her day at school. By chance a practice exam paper revealed Pia's strategy. She was then extremely upset and frightened that her parents and the teacher would be angry with her, and embarrassed about being revealed as "stupid".

Sometimes parents and carers have had difficulties with learning that were never recognized, and have endured stressful unsatisfactory days at school. It is not surprising that there are mixed feelings then about allowing others to identify their child as having a learning difficulty. Alternatively, the terms used can be distressing to adults: learning difficulties and specific needs can feel like a judgement that is fixed and discriminatory especially if they seem at odds with one's view of one's family history.

> Sandra's father had been a medical researcher, spending most of his working life studying and writing technical or academic papers. Sandra herself had followed in his footsteps, training as a doctor then specializing in cardiovascular diseases. She was dismayed to hear that her son Hugh had difficulty with maths and comprehending sequences of numbers. It seemed impossible that a child of hers could have this unexpected difficulty. So it took time for Sandra and her husband to accept that Hugh would need extra tuition to help him with his maths so that he could continue in his private school. Sandra was even more astonished when it was revealed some years later that she too had some difficulty with sequences, as she had been unaware of any particular frustration or inefficiency in processing information.

We often underestimate the degree of discomfort, shame even, that both children and their parents can feel about finding they may need particular help. Rather like a diagnosis from the doctor, the news can be met with a number of emotional responses, from relief to shame, and anxiety. As with other aspects of children's development, much can be done to help children by understanding that they may be anxious and upset about their experience before the problem was identified. It can also be of value to be able to discuss the matter with a professional who has experience of children's learning. Sometimes a child will be seen at school by an educational psychologist who has been specifically trained to assess and explore how children use their minds to learn. Educational psychologists have experience of many children and typical developments which they can apply to the individual child. This means that they can, if asked, explain what the nature of any difficulty might be and how it fits into the whole picture of a child's thinking and capacity to learn. Although they will write a report and make recommendations, parents and carers may have questions that they would like to ask directly. Sometimes, a psychologist will be preparing a statutory report at the request of the education department (a statement of educational needs in the UK). This usually follows a period of time during which teachers have been watching and considering how to help a child who is showing signs of needing more individually tailored support to learn, and as a contribution to their understanding, they will probably talk to parents to gather further information, or to share concerns. The amount of individually planned support offered to a child may vary according to the resources available in the local authority.

Special needs and disabilities

Children who are born with specific disabilities or who have developed a degree of physical or mental disability will need specialist support. At this age most children will have some established support, whether in the form of specialist schooling or treatment programmes. Parents may find it a painful decision to accept certain kinds of support, feeling that it increases the sense of their child as different or disabled. For example, making a choice between a specialist school, or keeping a youngster in a mainstream school, can be a trying and painful balancing task. The feelings and doubts mentioned above in connection with learning difficulties apply equally to the parents of a child with special needs. The extent to which a child of this age can cope with life in a mainstream school or manage taking part in a social life will depend as much on the feelings of both parents and child as it does on the actual physical or emotional symptoms of the disability. While some children will benefit from the specialist provision of a small school and feel happier mixing with children who understand more immediately their experience, others will need the sense of belonging and reassurance that comes from being able to socialize with children who have no specific disability. By having a close look at a child's outlook and personality as well as the details of the disability, it will be easier to come to conclusions about the kind of support that will help a child to thrive and fulfil his or her potential happily. It is also useful to be guided by one's intuition as a parent. This is important because the involvement of health or educational professionals can leave parents feeling that their understanding of their child is an amateur one, and therefore less significant than professional recommendations.

Disabling feelings

Apart from specific needs that arise from combinations of physical or constitutional factors, sometimes shocking events or unimagined distress can overtake us all. For the 10- and 11-year-old the impact of very strong feelings can lead to altered states of mind, just as an adult. Some of these events have already been discussed from the perspective of relatively typical family life and reasonable circumstances. Sometimes children do seem to become stuck, unable to free themselves from disabling thoughts, lying awake for many nights, plagued by the memory of nightmares. Sometimes relationships within the family are painful and difficult to negotiate. Children may, like adults, respond by becoming depressed and withdrawing from social contact. They may have disturbances of sleep or eating habits, or occasionally they may resort to hurting themselves as a salve to emotional distress. If it is not possible to help them through parental concern and support, the family doctor will be able to assess the severity of the problem and make a referral to a suitable clinician. It may involve a trip to meet a paediatrician in a hospital outpatient department, or a meeting with a family therapist to explore the concerns, or perhaps to a community service which has a team of professionals who are trained to give detailed consideration to a child's difficulties and decide on an appropriate treatment, if needed.

The onward journey

In this era, children are at a crossroads. The evidence of growth, and of time passing, highlighted by the arrival of that second digit to their age underlies an awareness of themselves as separate individuals. Whatever their circumstances, or whatever the characteristics of their personalities, they cannot avoid knowing that their days as helpless, dependent and inexperienced beginners are now numbered. As discussed in these pages, their response to this realization and their feelings about themselves and the world they inhabit may be infinitely varied. Inevitably the 11-year-old's view of the world he or she inhabits will be influenced by his or her experience of you as a parent or carer. Your continued interest, understanding and curiosity about your child, and your greater experience that can reassure and support him or her in times of difficulty, represents one of the most valuable assets he has in his growth towards adulthood.

Helpful Organizations

Bullying UK
185 Tower Bridge Road
London SE1 2UF
Tel: 020 7378 1446
www.bullying.co.uk
Advice for victims of bullying and their parents

ChildLine
45 Folgate Street
London E1 6GL
Tel: 020 7650 3200
Helpline: 0800 111 (for children and young people)
www.childline.org.uk
Confidential 24-hour helpline for children and young people

Exploring Parenthood
Latimer Education Centre
194 Freston Road
London W10 6TT
Tel: 020 8964 1827
Parents' Advice Line: 020 8960 1678
Advice on parenting problems from newborn to adult

Gingerbread Association for One Parent Families
7 Sovereign Close
London E1W 2HW
Tel: 020 7488 9300
Advice Line: 0800 018 4318 (Monday to Friday 9 a.m. to 5 p.m.)
www.gingerbread.org.uk
Support for single-parent families

Parentline Plus (formerly National Stepfamily Association)
Tel: 0808 800 2222 (helpline 24 hours a day)
www.parentlineplus.org.uk
Information and support for parents and stepparents

YoungMinds/National Association for Child and Family Mental Health
102–108 Clerkenwell Road
London EC1M 5SA
Tel: 020 7336 8445
Parents' Information Service: 0800 018 2138
www.youngminds.org.uk
Campaign to improve the mental health of children and young people

Recommended Reading

Bartram, P. (2007) *Understanding Your Young Child with Special Needs*. London: Jessica Kingsley Publishers.

Waddell, M. (2002) *Inside Lives: Psychoanalysis and the Development of Personality*. London: Karnac.

Wilson, J. (1992) *The Suitcase Kid*. London: Doubleday.

Wilson, J. (1997) *The Lottie Project*. London: Doubleday.

Winnicott, D. (1991) *The Child, the Family and the Outside World*. London: Penguin.

Index